Keith,

Thanks so much
for your support!

Shelley Hallmark

FINDING THE BALANCE

Insight to Understanding Life's Lessons

Shelley L. Hallmark

BALBOA.
PRESS

A DIVISION OF HAY HOUSE

Balboa Press books may be ordered through booksellers or by contacting:

Balboa Press
A Division of Hay House
1663 Liberty Drive
Bloomington, IN 47403
www.balboapress.com
1-(877) 407-4847

Because of the dynamic nature of the Internet, any Web addresses or links contained in this book may have changed since publication and may no longer be valid. The views expressed in this work are solely those of the author and do not necessarily reflect the views of the publisher, and the publisher hereby disclaims any responsibility for them.

The author of this book does not dispense medical advice or prescribe the use of any technique as a form of treatment for physical, emotional, or medical problems without the advice of a physician, either directly or indirectly. The intent of the author is only to offer information of a general nature to help you in your quest for emotional and spiritual well-being. In the event you use any of the information in this book for yourself, which is your constitutional right, the author and the publisher assume no responsibility for your actions.

Any people depicted in stock imagery provided by Thinkstock are models, and such images are being used for illustrative purposes only. Certain stock imagery © Thinkstock.

Printed in the United States of America

ISBN: 978-1-4525-3210-3 (sc)
ISBN: 978-1-4525-3212-7 (dj)
ISBN: 978-1-4525-3211-0 (e)

Library of Congress Control Number: 2011900041

Balboa Press rev. date: 01/31/2011

Little F.—"my biggest inspiration!"

My Mom – "for her endless support in my pursuit of happiness"

Friends and relationships are in your life for a reason, a season, or a lifetime.

I would be remiss if I didn't thank everyone who was and still is instrumental in my life. Without you, I wouldn't be who I am today.

PREFACE

Like many, I have struggled with the lessons in life that we are here to learn and grow from. Even though a lesson does not seem to be a blessing at the time it occurs, I can honestly say that without the lessons life has provided me with, I might not have gotten to where I am today.

If you think back upon every experience in your life and really examine each one, you will find that there is always an opportunity for personal growth. While you are in an event—whether it is pleasant or unpleasant—it is really hard to see and understand why that event is occurring. It is only after some time has passed that you can truly appreciate and learn from the experience itself.

I wish that all of us could learn from other's experiences, but unfortunately, that isn't always possible. Through this book, I am hoping that everyone finds at least one thing that they can take with them to enrich their life.

If you are able to enrich at least one person's life by being present in theirs then you have succeeded.

Contents

CHAPTER ONE

NEGATIVITY

egativity is one of the harder emotions to fight, and
it takes a great deal of inner strength to overcome it.
Negativity is not easily avoided, but it can be deflected
and defeated. You must refuse both emotional and physical
negativity. Emotional negativity can be thwarted by learning to
recognize the moment when a negative thought process begins to
enter your mind, cutting it off immediately, and replacing it with
the opposite positive thought. In other words, you must view the
glass as half-full instead of half-empty. For example, focus on
the negative aspects of a beautiful painting can be conquered by
looking for the hidden beauty that you might miss when only
taking a quick glance. Acknowledging all the work required to
create each individual brush stroke and how difficult it would be
for a beginner to attempt such a thing could also help you look
past superficial flaws to appreciate the beauty of the painting.
Once you train yourself to turn the negative into positive, you
will be surprised at how easy it is. Soon, the habit of looking for

flaws first will change. Your default way of thinking will begin to lean more towards the positive, thereby creating a much healthier thought process for your everyday life.

Others can also inflict negativity upon you. You need to protect yourself against this. When you begin to work to change your own thoughts, you will be more aware of negativity in others. One way to handle this is to excuse yourself from the negative person's presence. When people sound off about any topic, even though they aren't angry with you directly, they are conveying negativity. A day of running into five people like that can make you feel like you have five pianos tied to you. You become emotionally tired and drained; sometimes another person's negativity will cause you to feel negative about things. This is why deflecting negativity is important—so it won't rub off on you.

Once you've changed your own thought process and have begun to think only positive thoughts, the negative thoughts become things of the past, and you are better able to protect yourself. When others are inflicting negativity, you can easily counter their attitudes by keeping your mind strong and affirming the opposite as a positive in your mind. You don't need to berate another for their behavior. You can, however, point it out (if you feel so inclined) and move on. Not everyone is open to constructive advice. You are the better judge of those in your life and whether you need to censor your communications or not.

Physical negativity is behavior that enforces emotional negativity. When people become too interested in the personal lives of others, boundaries get crossed. Spreading gossip is the action that can sometimes precede the emotional pain that one feels from being the subject of gossip. The subject is then confronted by both the negative actions of others and their own emotional pain.

Negativity's sole purpose is to hurt others. It feeds and grows in very dark places—and like a virus, it makes people feel so awful that they pass it to others in an effort to alleviate their own sadness. Most of the time, negativity is passed on by the carrier, because they don't realize that the negativity they are spreading is actually connected to their own unhappiness. Unfortunately, the more they try to disperse that negativity, the more it comes back to them. This pattern can continue to go around in circles until one of two things happens: the person experiencing the negativity learns to recognize and deflect it, or they completely defeat it.

I realize that there is much negativity in this world, but I choose not to have it in my life. I choose to be happy. That being said, everyone—at some time or another—experiences the downside of negativity. There are low points in our lives when we don't have the energy to deflect or defeat negativity. One thing I can do at these times is to try to avoid projecting this negativity onto others. This may mean that I avoid interactions with others. When I can't, I do my best to bite my tongue, politely nod, and move on. Sometimes that's all I can do.

I've found that the more aware I became of others' desires to maintain the drama of unhappiness, the less it affects me because I realize it has nothing to do with me and more to do with what might be going on in their life. *Awareness* has been the key that has helped me to take a step back and not let the negativity of others infect me. I now recognize that these tests of negativity are their lessons to learn. Someone else's negativity has nothing to do with me. The more I understand this, the easier it is to create a barrier to protect myself. Awareness is power.

Thinking or saying something like, "If it weren't for bad luck, I wouldn't have any luck at all" has a way of determining the future. We do tend to get what we wish for. Thoughts are very powerful. Positive thoughts can help create positive change.

Negativity is very difficult to overcome. Some people use negativity to protect themselves from being hurt. They are not always willing to let go of the protective barrier they have erected to prevent personal hurt.

Sometimes negativity is about revenge for past hurts. It may not even be directed at the person it is being inflicted upon. Sometimes you just happen to be the one in the vicinity at the time. Remembering this when it happens is one way to realize the idea that awareness is power. If you can recognize what is really going on, try to introduce positive energy into the situation and leave. Negativity cannot survive in a positive environment. It either dissipates or has to move away. Darkness cannot survive in light; negativity cannot survive in the positive. When you introduce light into a negative environment, the negative person will either follow your lead and become more positive, or they will leave. Either way, you have chosen not to let negativity ruin your happiness.

CHAPTER TWO

MANIPULATION

Understanding manipulation is tough. Knowing how terrible I would feel if I had manipulated another person has always made it difficult for me to detect and accept that people willingly do it. I've always given others the benefit of the doubt—even when my gut told me otherwise. One of my biggest challenges was learning to listen to my gut instincts. Even though my instincts have never led me astray, my own ego-consciousness has. As it turns out, that was my weakest link.

Recognizing that I contributed to being manipulated is even more difficult to deal with than actually being manipulated. My contribution was not enforcing my boundaries and allowing someone else to control me. Avoiding being manipulated by others involves learning from the past. This means understanding not only why something happened but also why I was blind enough to allow it.

You know the routine! Many people today are still experiencing this sort of subtle deception. Why?

Everyone comes into this life with lessons to learn. Some lessons are harder than others, but one thing is the same—and that is that all the lessons learned help us to experience personal growth and shape us into the people we are meant to be. I have often asked myself, "What possible path could I be meant for that would require me to be manipulated by others?" Well, one very good possible reason would be that I wouldn't be able to share my experience with you, and if I didn't have this very valuable insight, then my writing here would be lacking a vital part. Based on my own personal nature as I know it, I might also have experienced the manipulation on a smaller scale then what might have happened in my later years, which could have been quite catastrophic.

If, however, we do not learn one of life's lessons the first time, we will keep repeating that lesson until we do learn it. I can honestly say that I've had the displeasure of not learning the first time around—and when the lesson came around again, the experience was stronger and harder to deal with. After going through the difficult emotions again, I wished I had learned my lesson the first time; but I'm glad that I at last learned. I think the components and severity of the situations increase with each time the lesson repeats itself.

The hardest thing to get past when you have been subjected to manipulation is the shame and guilt you put on yourself. As hard as it is at that time to look ahead, it's better to realize that we are human, and at one time or another, we might be taken advantage of—for no other reason than the learning experience itself. Think of it as being a creative mistake. We all create what we want; sometimes we make errors. It just means we go back to the drawing board and create to our liking.

We need to learn not to judge ourselves so harshly. I know this is a hard task—I still struggle with it, although not as much as I used to. Wisdom and time have taught me that I am not to blame—but rather that I need to strengthen and enforce my boundaries.

I was quite ego-conscious from the first time I experienced manipulation, and I thought that it wasn't going to happen to me again—lesson learned. How wrong I was when it came around a second time.

When we don't understand or learn a lesson the first time, we tend to blame ourselves. The idea here is not to blame yourself. Believe me; I know that is a hard request! Instead, focus your energy on figuring out why you allowed the manipulation to happen and how to recognize and prevent it in the future.

Did you allow yourself to be manipulated because of a greater need for something else you wanted, and even though the package wasn't perfect, it would do, because you were growing impatient? Don't sell what you deserve and need short. Never settle! Everything that you desire is available—you must maintain your vision and focus on attaining it.

If you find that there are people in your life who are constantly draining your spirit and emotional state of mind, it might be time to reassess what contribution or effect (positive or negative) they are having on your life. Within every relationship, there should be an equal exchange of give and take—and that applies to the very innermost desires of your soul. No one person deserves or should be subjected to anything less than that. Your inner soul's needs are the most important needs to be met. If your soul is injured, that injury affects everything in your body and everyone in your life. Your soul's needs aren't just for your own happiness, but for your existence as well.

Please do not continually beat yourself up about why something has turned out the way it has. There is no benefit to doing that—benefits lie within changing actions in the future, and that is something to take pride in. If nothing else, you can create a more prosperous and happy future. What could be a better outcome than that?

As difficult and emotionally draining as some of these lessons can be, without them, we will never reach our ultimate goals. What is your ultimate goal? Well, that is different for every individual, and it depends on the lessons we chose to learn. You may notice that many people have relayed the experience that doors just opened for them, they were led to a certain outcome, and things just flowed. I think when you experience the path of least resistance, everything will just flow—and that is how you know you are on the right path. When you are on the right path, you will prosper in contentment, faith, abundance, and acceptance.

The reason a positive person experiences life as they do is because they have chosen to create a more prosperous and happy future. This is the result of changing how you view things—you are able to interpret and affect the outcome of a situation.

My two hardest subjects to write about are negativity and manipulation—mostly because I don't like to give a lot of energy to either of these. It's not that I don't think these feeling, important part of creating who we are as people; it's just that there is no benefit to focusing too much energy on negative emotions. Yes, some of us have to learn about them the hard way—but once the lessons are learned, what results is a positive outcome. I've found that often when others are relaying hard times, they usually have a success story that has come from it—the success being that they got through the difficult time and were better for it.

Really, though, if we learn to take a step back and try to make a positive assessment, things might seem a little less stressful on our minds and hearts.

Dwelling on things in the past will only keep the source of the negative energy within you—and that, of course, will keep it in your mind and in your life forever.

CHAPTER THREE

DISCRIMINATION

I t's unfortunate that even with all the advances we have made, we still experience discrimination. Who is anyone to judge?

Discrimination comes in many forms, but they all types of discrimination have one thing in common—people are judging others based on their own sense of what is considered valuable. Who do these people think they, are and what gives them the right to determine the self-worth of others?

This is an ego-related thought process—an "I'm better than you" attitude. Sometimes this attitude is born from a false sense of superiority, for whatever reason such as money or stature. It can also come from intense insecurity—sometimes people will attack others in an effort to make themselves feel more worthy.

Another source of discrimination is bad experiences—and those experiences are then held against anyone who bears a similarity to the negative experience. These bad experiences can also be passed on from others. Your environment in your formative childhood years plays a major part in who you are. Sometimes our families and friends can be the instigators of our biggest lessons and the causes of some of our not-so-great traits. People don't just grow up with discrimination inside them; it takes conditioning of some sort, and it can take a lot of work to turn this kind of negativity around. People don't want to readily let their discriminatory attitudes go.

Feelings like discrimination can become protective barriers to many. When people project this negativity onto others, it takes the focus off of them and can become a defense mechanism. An example of this is the child on the playground who feels picked and then finds someone they believe to be of lesser stature to pick on. Discrimination can be, like negativity, a shield to hide behind—and there are more people than you would think who actually hide behind these shields.

If you are one of the people hiding behind this type of shield, then you know that without your shield, you can feel completely exposed and very vulnerable.

The effect of this shielding is that others will not get to know the true person behind the shield. In an effort to protect ourselves, we have also distanced ourselves from having very real and honest relations with others that could possibly provide much more reward and happiness than hiding.

I have noticed that some people put themselves in a never-ending cycle of unhappiness—not because they don't want happiness, but because on some level, they feel they don't deserve it. This couldn't be further from the truth. Sometimes we judge ourselves too harshly—

The people I have come across who feel they don't deserve happiness end up continually pushing away any people or situations that could result in happiness, because experiences from their past that have left them feeling unworthy or unloved. They sabotage their own happiness because of this. These people are unhappy with how their lives are turning out, but they do not seem to realize that they are the cause of their continued heartache. I think that on some level, they know this, but attribute their unhappiness to the idea that what life is actually bringing to them is what they deserve. This could not be further from the truth; they themselves are attracting unhappiness. The people I've known who do this to themselves don't deserve their unhappiness as much as they think they do.

On the flip side of this, there are people who don't judge themselves harshly enough and take advantage of others without feeling remorse. Surprisingly, these people are the ones who judge others harshly, although they seem to act without conscience. It's been my experience that the people who continually punish themselves are the ones who are committing the lesser evils compared to the ones with the over-inflated egos.

Some people are discriminated against because of what they own (or don't own). How can anyone's self-worth be determined by any material object? A person's character is what matters and just because someone has more possessions than another does not mean that they are better than anyone else. You can't take your net worth with you when you leave this world, can you? What good is that net worth going to do for you on the other side? I can tell you—nothing! You will realize this when you get to the other side.

This is a difficult subject for me to tackle, because I have strong empathy for those who have to endure adversity. Whether that adversity is due to a person's level of education, culture, age, skin color, gender, or sexual orientation, these attributes shouldn't be barriers in any way, shape, or form. Everyone deserves the same opportunities for happiness, and everyone should be respected in spite of their different beliefs. We connect with others through the soul, and souls bear no differences. If you refuse to connect with someone because of your own ignorance, you are cutting yourself off from an opportunity that could be truly inspiring. There are many people that I have come across that have inspired more than I could have ever imagined and if I had chosen not to connect with any one of them I would have deprived myself of some very unexpected inspiration.

CHAPTER FOUR

RESPECT

Respect seems to be in a state of transition these days

The only way to help others change is through positive influence, not harsh words or actions. The phrase "you catch more flies with honey than vinegar" captures this idea perfectly. Others rarely respond to negative communication, whether it is through words or actions. Most people are drawn to the positive, because there are so many things in this crazy world that cause unhappiness or are out of balance. So it makes sense that happy encounters are the most likely to be sought after.

It can be so disappointing at times that basic respect seems to have become so lost.

Respect others—and if you can't respect them, then move yourself elsewhere.

Everyone deserves respect—even when they are behaving in a way that is not in alignment with how you view basic respect. It is still not your place to judge someone who is disrespectful. You should only be judging your own behavior and adjusting it according to how you would like to be treated. If others respect behaviors aren't acceptable to you that is their issue—but you do not need to tolerate any behavior that doesn't line up with your own outlook. The best way I have found to deal with a disrespectful attitude is to move myself away from a situation where this attitude is present.

Everyone is here to learn their own lessons. If you encounter someone whose behavior challenges your boundaries on respect, then maybe that is that person's chosen lessons to learn, overcome, and grow from; maybe you are the one placed in their life to let them know how they are affecting others around them. We are not here to tell others how they should behave; we can only offer a positive influence. It's not that we don't have time to help others—we have our own lessons to learn at different times, and like others, at some times we are open and at other times we are not.

Communication with others can be a big hurdle. I've learned that I should take a moment to tell someone how I understand something they say to me. For instance, if I hear something a certain way, it doesn't mean that's what someone was trying to get across to me—that's just how I've interpreted it. My idea of better communication is to tell the person how I perceive what they are saying and how it affects me. By doing this, I give that person the opportunity to re-clarify and understand how they are directly affecting me. No one can read minds, and everyone's mind processes differently—so it makes sense that others might not interpret your words to have the same meaning as what you are saying to them.

If you learn to communicate with others, then you give both yourself and the person you are speaking to a better course of communication, thus making your relations that much better.

Your beliefs are truly your own, and every person has the right to their own beliefs. If someone else's beliefs are different then yours, it does not mean that you should force them to see things your way. We align ourselves with others who compliment us, share with us, and oppose us. We need the balance of all these things—that way life doesn't become predictable.

You need to acknowledge that everyone is (unique) and that we are all allowed to have our own dreams—whatever those dreams may be. The goal should be to reach contentment in your soul by reaching for what you want as an individual. There is no rule book or guideline to state what that should be—you will know what you want by paying attention to how you feel inside and seeing what resonates within you. Your life goals should not be based on what someone out there says is or is not normal.

I think when others are trying to impose their views of what "normal thinking" is, it's because they feel they know what's right for others. Sometimes the thought is appreciated—but sometimes it is not. I've been guilty of doing this—imposing ideas on others, even though I've done this it's still not my place.—If I feel that if I don't ask for someone's opinion or advice, then they should keep their thoughts to themselves and I should do the same

I myself can become stubborn when unsolicited advice comes my way, but I've learned to just thank others for their ideas and move on. There is no need to debate things unnecessarily—especially when you know that no good will come from it.

It seems crazy that society as a whole has this idea that a happy life is supposed to be "one size fits all." That is just perception. If that were the case, our society wouldn't be as diverse as it is. Culturally we have made a lot of progress; that is obvious, based on how different the world is today compared to how it was thirty years ago. We are becoming more open to others of different cultures, skin color, gender, and sexual orientation—and we should. There should never have been any barriers to begin with. Everyone in this world deserves a chance to be as great as they can be.

We are becoming more open to topics that were taboo in the past. For example, if anyone mentioned anything to do with the psychic world thirty years ago, that was considered crazy. Now we are welcoming topics like these in varying degrees.

You are on your own spiritual journey, and every person and event comes into your life for a reason. Some people or events are more significant than others, but all things happen for a greater purpose. We all have lessons to learn and growth to experience. How would we ever achieve this learning or growth without challenges? It is not our right to judge others by what lessons they are here to learn or what mistakes they might make along the way—just as no one else has the right to judge us.

When you are aligned with someone who is important to you on a soul level, it is through that person's actions, words, or mere presence that you experience a connection. There is no chance of missing this connection when it happens—you will feel it within your heart.

When you start to align yourself with others who do not share your sense of self, integrity, and values, then you need to question why.

In case you can't tell, I was blessed with a mother who taught me many things. She has taught me grace, respect, love, appreciation, gratitude, and faith, and she has given me constant, unconditional support. If I can be even half the woman she is, I will be truly blessed.

CHAPTER FIVE

CONFIDENCE

L ack of confidence can be a big obstacle, and there are many traits that stem from it. For example, when people lack confidence, one thing that results is low self-esteem. It is that low self-esteem that can produce bad treatment of others. The act of treating others poorly leads to guilt and shame, which then creates a greater lack of confidence and an increase in low self-esteem.

People who lack confidence and have low self-esteem are likely to make bad decisions—for no other reason than that somewhere along the way, someone else made them feel like they didn't matter or that what they had to offer didn't matter.

Don't let others decide for you what your own self-worth is. We all have a purpose—it doesn't matter if that purpose is great or small. We are all an intricate part of the big wheel.

ost surprising thing to me happens when I think I have someone figured out—then they do something that completely shocks me. Sometimes they do something good, and sometimes what they do is not so good. Nonetheless, it is very humbling, because it is at that time that I realize I had misjudged the person.

The key word being judged and at that point realizing that as much as I express that we aren't here to judge others, sometimes we do it unconsciously. I have to pay attention to my thoughts and always work towards changing my own thought process. It does get easier to recognize and divert my thoughts from judging others.

When your confidence in your own ability to read people is affected, you should remember that you are wired to trust your own inner truths. Someone who is confident in themselves is not going to have a problem trusting their own instincts.

Control over others is another trait that is a result of a lack of confidence. People who have not been allowed to have a voice in their own lives for a long period of time can develop a tendency to try to control others of as a means of regaining the strength they felt was taken away.

Everyone has something to offer; everyone in your life is there for a reason. It is up to you to grasp the lessons you should learn from the people in your life, the influence of others, and roles each person plays in your life.

I'm not saying you have to spend all your time examining what each person's place in your life is; I just believe you should appreciate the greater purpose of others, honor that purpose, and then have confidence in yourself. We all have a place in this world, and each person can make a difference—whatever that difference may be.

I've been amazed many times by how wrong I have been about others. Sometimes I have been terribly disappointed by others; and at other times, I have been happily surprised—but above all else, I realize that if I had just had confidence in my own assessments, I might not have had to experience the surprise or the disappointment.

The habit of judging others is hard to overcome, but it is necessary to our overall personal development. I have prematurely judged people only to find out that I was very wrong. This is not to say that we are to travel through life slap-happy, letting others walk all over us. We still need to be cognizant of personalities that aren't in alignment with ours on a soul level. Our egos and lack of confidence overrule our soul's instincts, because our ego tells us, "I know better."

If you are unhappy with any part of your life, then the solution is to change it to your liking. There isn't anything that you can't do or accomplish. Things become too big to tackle only because you make it that way in your mind. Break things down, tackle them one at a time, or do them all at once—the best method of dealing with tasks depends on your personality type, what you are comfortable with, and what you are able to adapt to. You can change anything you want to your liking—I wholeheartedly believe this. I know it, I've seen it done, and I've done it—the key is to have unshakeable confidence in yourself. Take a look back on your life, be thankful for what you have come through so far, and be optimistic about what's to come. We all have our own inner strength—we just need to believe in ourselves.

I've seen and read many success stories of people who have accomplished great things, and they were able to attain great things because they worked hard and were determined to make a change.

Those who don't have the true desire to be where they say they want to be are where they are for a reason—it may be a lack of confidence, low self-esteem, or an inability to let go of the shield that protects them from experiencing life fully.

It has taken me forty years to realize that I am a disabler. I enable others so much that I end up disabling them. It is a good thing to support others in their ambitions and desires—but when you do everything for them, that is going too far. As generous as it may seem, it is also too much.

You have to give others the chance to develop and maintain their own confidence and self-esteem. If they don't take care of themselves, they will feel inferior and otherwise disabled—and you yourself might risk feeling resentful and unappreciated. People come to expect you to maintain that disabling behavior once you begin to enable them.

When you determine your level of expectations of others, you should make sure your expectations are the same for everyone. There are no special cases; everyone should be respected and treated equally. If you discover that you have different expectations for different people, then take a look within to see if you mig overcompensating for something you feel you lack.

A person who has a generous heart is usually too kind to be strict and ends up being a doormat for the wicked. Some people use kindness to exert control over others—for example, when they give gifts, those gifts are later used as tools to make demands or exact guilt. This is not to say that every person who performs an act of kindness has ill intent—this is just another perspective to consider. The best strategy for dealing with like these is to examine all your personal relationships with others and what type of boundaries and dynamics are active in the healthy relationships as opposed to the unhealthy relationships. This might help you to either redirect into a more positive relationship or determine that it is time for you to move on.

CHAPTER SIX

RESISTANCE

We all have the choice to take what we want from any relationship—good or bad. Since bad things have always caused me unhappiness, I choose to take good things—but I try to learn at least one thing from each bad experience.

I have found that the hardest emotion to let go of is resentment. Resentment is created by anger, which is why it is so hard to let go of. Anger has a way of continuing to fester within you and can do much damage to your psyche and soul. Anger is one of the emotions that is most necessary to get rid of because of this—and it is because of our own resistance that we sometimes refuse to let our anger go. It actually takes a lot more of your energy to resist letting go of anger and resentment than to accept life as it comes.

Holding on to resentment isn't worth it—especially when it comes to the people that matter the most. Holding on to resentment

27

actually isn't worth it at all—no matter who has acted against you or what they've done. In reality, you aren't really holding on to the anger; you're holding on to the hurt.

Once I had realized that holding on to these types of negative emotions was doing me more harm than good, the decision to release it all was the first step—and really, that's the biggest part of the battle. It's the *aha* moment—like when an addict hits rock bottom and finally decides to get help. The realization and admission are the rock bottom of this scenario. The next step can be one of many. If you are holding on to hurt caused by another person, you can choose to talk to them and tell them how they have affected you, or you can talk about it with someone you trust. Either way, you need to release the negativity—get it off your chest. I promise you that this exercise alone will take a significant weight of stress off of you, and you will feel better. You have a choice as to which way you choose to release it. Whatever you choose will alleviate the burden, but one might take longer than another. If you choose to talk with a trusted friend, then you will receive an opinion from someone who is not emotionally connected to the situation that is causing you the hurt—a fresh perspective. A friend can offer you input, if you so desire—or they can just listen.

If you choose to talk out your negative experience with the source of your hurt, then things might be resolved more quickly for you. In talking things out, you are offering the person insight into how they have affected you (and possibly others), as well as the chance to correct or retract their actions or words. You might find that how you have been affected might not have mattered to them at all—but either way, you will get closure, and this is the key. It is not good for anyone to dwell on things of the past. The only person affected by the past is you—and in a negative way.

There is no greater healing process than letting that which does not serve any purpose go. No matter which way you choose to do it, as long as you release your negative feelings, that's all that matters.

The ego can be hard to overrule—especially when you hold things in instead of releasing them into the universe. The ego can hold on to emotions associated with disappointment, anger, and sadness; those emotions can swirl around inside your mind and body and cause very negative things to happen. Things like disease can be created from negative emotions, because when your mind is in a state of negativity, there is nothing positive reinforcing the protection of your body.

Now along this line of thinking, I've often wondered why some children are afflicted with very real diseases—like cancer, for example—as they do not have the ego-related issues that we as adults experience. I have watched documentaries of families that have gone through this kind of experience, and almost all of these families end up creating a positive effect from these experiences. No matter what the outcome of their child's health these parents have moved on to bringing greater awareness and it's from their actions that others lives are affected in a positive way. It was through their child that they were inspired and motivated to create these positive actions.

These experiences—whether they ended happily or sadly—all have one thing in common, and that is that the families involved have gained a tremendous amount of insight into the greater meaning behind their experience and all of them relay the positive influence that these children have had on their lives. Even if the children were only in the family members' lives for a short time, the families find appreciation and gratitude for the child's life, and that is very inspiring. Even though these situations are extremely difficult and sad, somehow these people look for and find the positive in them—which is really the greater purpose. These children were placed in these family members' lives to teach them lessons that they are here to learn.

I remember watching one of these shows and it told the story somewhat like the following . It was about a woman who was an extremely negative person and her beautiful child becomes afflicted with cancer. There was nothing she felt she could do, so she placed her anger on life and how awfully unfair it was. Of course, this would be a typical reaction; I would expect that I would also have these thoughts as well. These thoughts aren't wrong; they are just a likely part of the process.

The child, being so innocent ends up giving the parent the biggest blessing by being in their life and ends up reassuring them not to be angry. Here the child is, in the biggest battle of their tiny life, and they are coaching the parent and displaying more strength than the parent had ever expected. This ends up teaching the parent a deeper appreciation for their child—and how could the parent not learn to display the very same strength that their child has so innocently shown them?

These lessons don't always come in the form we might have expected them to—but God has a plan for us all, and every single thing in your life happens for a reason. If you look closely enough, you will find the positive in every situation.

When others do wrong by you, you may develop a wall of protection—and the more walls you create, the harder it becomes for anyone to really get to know you; obviously, this makes socializing very difficult. Sometimes you can create an alternate form of yourself to cope with the fear of such socialization or closeness. If you never really let anyone in, then they can't hurt you—or at least, that's the defense mechanism. The longer this goes on, the sicker your soul becomes—and at some point, you've become so far removed from yourself that you don't know who you really are anymore.

The more this happens, the more secluded, antisocial, and sick you become. However, society is making great strides to become more aware of this, and people are making much effort to improve their quality of lives and live with greater enlightenment. This is evident, because we are starting to pay attention to our challenges, learn from them, talk about them, and experience personal growth. We are looking for a greater meaning and happiness within.

There are still some people who are stuck in the growth process— but I have noticed that people aren't feeding those emotions as much as they used to. People are finding their own way to move away from negativity—whether through deflection or just letting it go.

CHAPTER SEVEN

GRATITUDE/APPRECIATION

Sometimes the lines are a little blurred when it comes to gratitude and appreciation; understanding the difference can be difficult to decipher and a little confusing at times.

Without appreciation, you may take things for granted and turn them into expectations—things you think we are entitled to. The only thing you are entitled to is your own happiness, and that is something that only you can create. Upon creating your own happiness, you will experience soul evolution. Entitlement is something your ego has created. As horrifying as some people's actions can be, you should be able to find greater appreciation within the experience. I will use my own personal example. My daughter was three and a half months premature; she had many challenges to overcome just to live. It was hard for me to yield to the doctors and not be able to care for and protect my daughter the way a mother should. All I was able to provide for her was my strength and support—and I know that she felt it, because she flourished and exceeded the expectations the doctors had for her progress.

I also had to acknowledge and appreciate the greater force around me that was blessing me with her presence. In addition to that, I was given the opportunity to witness a miracle—and how could I not acknowledge and appreciate that? When I look back now and think about all the challenges she overcame, how could I not admire the strength of this tiny being? She overcame more challenges in the first three months of her life than adults might ever have to even attempt. For someone who started out so little, she proved to many that the strength of the soul can accomplish anything. Anyone who has love and support around them can overcome all sorts of adversity.

My daughter and I share a very close bond; it's based on a mutual strength we provide for each other. As terrifying as it was to go through her medical complications at the time, we went through it together—and we are stronger and closer because of it. Life had given me quite a challenge, and because of that challenge, I was given the opportunity to be stronger than I had ever imagined.

My daughter is a young girl now, and I find that she inspires me in many ways every day. She still has challenges ahead of her, but she handles them all in an effortless and positive way. I can't help but to admire who she is now and who she will become.

As life continues to go on, we sometimes lose sight of the things we need to be most appreciative of—but if we are lucky, we will notice what we have to be thankful for every day.

Instead of focusing on what you don't have, focus more on what you do have. Start by trying to find at least one thing you have to be thankful for each day. Why is that we designate only one day of the year to acknowledge and appreciate the things in our lives?

Gratitude is a little different from appreciation—while people can be appreciative of certain events, they sometimes aren't grateful for the entirety of it all. My own analogy of this is that gratitude is a puzzle, and every piece of the puzzle is a piece of appreciation.

What matters is not how things really are, but rather, how you choose to look at things. Everything that happens in your life is an opportunity, and the opportunity lies with your perception. You can either choose to see the negative aspects of a situation and determine from that what you lack, or you can choose to see the positive.

Some people spend an entire lifetime continually making the same mistakes, never learning from them, placing blame onto others, and never being grateful.

Every cloud has a silver lining, and if you choose to look at it any other way, then you are depriving yourself of true happiness. Mistakes are opportunities to go back and fine-tune something to your liking. The fact of the matter is that you do have options; that in itself is something to be grateful for.

Looking back on some of the events in my life, I can say without a doubt that some were emotionally draining, but every event helped me to create a strength of character I didn't realize I had. Some of the events prompted me to take a more active role in creating the kind of future I wanted—a future I might not have had the motivation to create otherwise.

It is with gratitude and love that I write everything contained in this book. One thing I have noticed is how somber my environment becomes when a tragedy occurs in the world. When tragedies caused by nature occur, people reflect on their own mortality, slow down, and appreciate what they have in the moment. It's unfortunate that our hectic and busy lives don't allow us a time-out more often to live in gratitude and love, but if nothing else, we can find this positive in these senseless disasters like the tsumani in Thailand, Hurricane Katrina, or just recently the earthquake in Haiti. It's just my opinion, but it's an example of drastic times calling for drastic measures. When this world becomes too crazily obsessed and ego-boosted, it seems that disasters like these create an extreme, worldwide wake-up call—something we desperately need at times when we are losing touch with the deeper meaning of reasons for being.

Life isn't about how much stuff or money you can attain. These things don't determine any worth except to the ego. You can't take any of your things with you when you go, and they don't determine that you get a first class ride all the way to the afterlife, because there are no ratings there.

My meaning in life and my level of wealth aren't based on net worth, money, or stuff, but rather on quality and contentment. Luxury to me is quality time with my family and friends—people who touch my heart and nourish my soul. That is something I can enjoy here and take with me when I go.

When you nourish your soul with the things that bring about contentment, that satisfaction is automatically transmitted outward, creating a gentle and loving atmosphere around you.

CHAPTER EIGHT

FAITH

H aving faith can at times be a hard task. When things aren't going your way, it can be very hard to have faith that things will work out for the best. Where you stumble in this is allowing your egos to tell you that you know best how things are supposed to work out—and when things don't go the expected way, you get discouraged. Your ego causes you to create unrealistic expectations at times—and it's these expectations that challenge your faith.

Struggling to understand is one of the hardest tasks. Putting energy into believing in yourself is vital. You have to learn to train yourself to recognize when you turn down the wrong path and have the ability to re-direct yourself back. You can have anything you want if you open yourself to receive all the blessings that life has to offer.

When you feel trapped by your thoughts and you pray for guidance or a sign, you need to be open to receiving that direction. Signs don't always come in the form you expect them—so in order to get the answers you seek, you need to expand your awareness.

Imagine that you are looking for guidance in a problem. You turn on the television, and someone is speaking on that particular subject. Or you may encounter someone who unknowingly provides you with the wisdom you're looking for. You could turn on the radio, and the song playing could take you back to a certain time in your life when the problem you are experiencing would never have bothered you—or a time in which there was a situation you overcame, which reminds you of how to proceed.

I'm sure by now you are getting the gist of what I am saying. All of these circumstances are examples of the signs you might receive. They are probably not in the format you expected to receive them, but they are signs nonetheless, because they have provided you with the answers to your requests. This is why I say you need to expand your awareness. You need to be fully open to receiving, and you can be guaranteed you will be given what you need. Gifts like these come in many different forms; it is your job to interpret them and apply what you have learned to your life. Remember that everything happens for a reason.

Sometimes it can be quite difficult to figure out what the underlying reason is for the occurrences you experience—but that is the challenge. Life isn't supposed to be easy; if it was easy, you would be bored. If you look back on the challenges you have experienced, you might find that many of them occurred because life became too mundane and you were bored. Some people desire a routine; others seek adventure.

There are downfalls to both outlooks on life. The people who like routine could get bored; the people seeking adventure could take unfathomable risks. So the question is this: do you stand in the fire or outside of it? The answer is within you. I like to be somewhere in between; that is my comfort level. Each person has their own individual comfort level, and each person must determine what that is. Only you hold the answers to your deepest desires.

Your heart holds the secrets to your inner desires. You need to connect your soul to those desires—and all of those desires do not have to be just dreams. You can make anything you want happen—just believe!

Here is something to think about—it's been noted that we as humans only use ten percent of our brains. Now with that ten percent, many people have created incredible changes. Imagine if we all were to tap in to access more than that ten percent—what could we create?

Your mind is the most powerful tool you have available. Your mind is not something material that you have to buy. It's available to you every single day. Think back and try to remember any event in your life where there was something you wanted deeply to create. You focused all your energy on positive reinforcement. Were you able to create or attain what you wanted? Most likely you were—but on the off chance you weren't, you should be able to identify what inhibited it.

As an adult, you still have a version of your younger self inside you, holding on to the dreams you had as a child—it's just that sometimes you lose faith. Why is that? As you get older, your dreams may change. The dreams you have as an adult might not necessarily be the dreams you sought as a child—but there is still emotion attached to those dreams. As time goes by, you may put constraints and limits on your dreams and tell yourself you can no longer achieve them—which is completely ridiculous! Your hopes suffer as well, and without the unadulterated passion you had when you were a child, your dreams are drastically diminished.

I would rather maintain my faith then invest my thoughts into the world when it seems so crazy—and I think that there are plenty of people out there who want to create the same positive change that I want. I see little signs of this almost daily now. That is a large step up from how things have been in the past, because there were times when I couldn't even find one positive thing in an entire week. Maybe I wasn't paying enough attention, or maybe I wasn't living in gratitude. I can't say for sure—but I do know that I would rather look for positive things than negative ones, and it seems to me that there are many people also looking for that. Like attracts like—think about that! More people thinking positively means more positive things will happen—we are creating positive change together.

Bring back your dreams, wishes, hopes, and faith. Dare to accomplish what you have always wanted. There are many people out there now doing just that—living their dreams.

It never hurts to try to accomplish your dream—and I would rather get to the end of my life saying, "I tried it; it wasn't for me" than wondering, "what if?" No one is too old or too far gone in their ways to try to achieve something they've always wanted.

I'm sure everyone has heard someone say that if anyone had told them any number of years ago that they would be where they are, they wouldn't have believed that person—and that's because their egos would never have dreamed the thing that had actually happened. Blind faith means believing that everything will work out the way it's meant to—and you don't always know what is meant to be.

Faith isn't something you can see or touch; it's something you feel within. Your instincts will tell you when you are on the right path—and from there, everything just flows; there are no obstacles.

One of the things I have to absolutely point out is that as much as relationships can hurt, sometimes you need to take the leap to try to make a relationship work. If you close yourself off, thinking that you can protect yourself with a wall and not get hurt, that is true—but you also cut yourself off from experiencing wonderful emotions and connections.

Without an uninhibited leap of faith, you may protect yourself from hurt—but you're also protecting yourself from happiness. You need these experiences to shape who you will become. Even though you don't see it at the time, everything will become clear. There is a greater purpose behind everything. You just have to believe!

Without the many pleasant and unpleasant experiences I have had, I might not have written this book. It's through this creative outlet that I get to really express myself and feel a greater sense of self-worth.

Do you realize that you can turn your entire life around in two years? I'll give you an example of inhibiting your own dreams. When I was a teenager, I always thought that I wanted to be a singer—but I held myself back in fear. If I had wanted to sing as much as I thought I did, nothing would have stopped me. In later years, I still wanted that dream—but I replaced the fear with a whole new set of reasons as to why I was stuck where I was. You may notice that I put a ceiling on myself—one that had no reason to be there.

Just try thinking back to find where you might have at one time blocked yourself in the past.

Another thing to recognize is that everyone is here for a reason. We all have things to accomplish and bring to this world. For every bad thing that happens, something good is created. Without grief and pain, we wouldn't develop compassion or forgiveness. The situations necessary to create these learning experiences are not ideal, but they are necessary.

Everyone in this world has a contribution to make—whether it's big or small is no matter. An example of this is a man we'll call Tom. Tom is a big-time stockbroker who has worked hard to get where he is and has no respect for anyone who doesn't push themselves to have high-stature careers. The only thing missing in Tom's life is someone to share his success with. Tom is looking for love, and had made this request to the universe. Every day, Tom leaves his office and walks down the street to where his car is parked and is usually annoyed by the panhandlers on the street. This particular day, he sees one homeless man who draws his attention—and he has no idea why. The man is not bothering him the way the others usually do; he is just keeping to himself. For the first time, Tom is really seeing someone. Tom passes the homeless man, but then turns back—Tom just feels he must do something positive, whether it's speaking a kind word or giving a couple dollars. This homeless man has made an impact on Tom, unbeknownst to either man. The homeless man expresses gratitude for Tom's interest, and it makes Tom feel great inside.

A month later, Tom meets a woman whose career is working with the homeless. This is a career Tom had previously looked down upon, but due to his earlier encounter with the homeless man, Tom's view has finally changed, creating the alignment within his life to his inner heart's desire.

Not all life events happen this way, but Tom's story is a good example of recognizing the signs. Tom was asking the universe to bring him love; yet he wasn't fully open to receive it. This homeless man helped to create awareness in Tom that was the prelude to creating that opening. Tom had blocked himself with ignorance—with something that was not his place to judge. By letting go of the hot coal of ignorance in his hand, Tom opened himself to receive the happiness he had sought.

Every time I have experienced change—whether that change has been positive or negative—it has created the anticipation of not knowing what's to come. With every change, greater things have come my way—not because of anything other than my faith, and my faith has never taken me down the wrong road. The times when I have gone down the wrong road have been times when I abandoned my faith—when I felt I knew better.

My only intent with this book is to open others to look within themselves, learn how to create positive change, and pass this gift on to the people in their lives. If everyone was to live their life positively, think of how much change the human race could make. We need adversity to keep things interesting—but why should adversity be so negatively damaging that we can't make a difference?

I've found in the last few years that my beliefs and faith have been challenged and changed. For a while, I was so disappointed in people I had believed in that I felt like giving up on people entirely. But I found that slowly, my faith came back—and this happened through the most unexpected sources.

What I've learned is that while my faith has changed, it has changed for the better. I used to walk around blindly, thinking that if individuals were given certain opportunities, they would change their circumstances. But what I've learned is that if people want to change their lives for the better, they will—for no other reason than because they wanted to.

Opportunity does not determine this if someone changes their circumstances —it is your inner motivation and desire that makes the difference. I'm not saying that you still can't believe—but don't sell the farm to try to create an opportunity for someone, they need to feel worthy and strong enough to create their own change of circumstance..

At times I have been saddened by the many things happening in this world, and it will take many of us to change the world. There are many people who are already making a positive difference, and I know that we all have something unique to contribute. I see evidence of that daily.

CHAPTER NINE

FORGIVENESS/COMPASSION

Forgiveness is needed for your own inner peace. It is important to let go of negative feelings that can wreak havoc within your body. If you haven't noticed this, then give forgiveness a try. When you hold on to negative emotions, you aren't hurting or even affecting the person those emotions are directed at—you are ultimately only hurting yourself. Like attracts like—put energy into negativity, and you will attract more negativity.

You need to find a healthy way to release your negativity into the universe so it doesn't burn you up inside. In the past, if I felt upset with someone, I would write a letter but never send it. This way I would get everything out I needed to. It would make me feel better, because the negative emotions were out of my system, and I didn't lower myself on any level to deal with them.

I know that this can be very hard to do, but try not to let others' negative emotions impact your own happiness. When you allow that to happen, you are giving others control over your life. When people feel like they have been unjustly served, they tend to inflict their unhappiness onto others—not intentionally, but only because they too need to let it out. This is an example of how negativity can cause people to have many internal problems. Think of your body as being like a pinball machine, with negativity as the ball. If you don't let your negative feelings out, they will continually move around, causing you to feel awful everywhere they hit within you. This is a very crude example, but it is the best analogy, because it gives you a visual idea of the effects.

Negativity does not only affect you; you might also pass it on to others. Negativity is like a virus in your system. It does not belong there, which is why it makes you behave differently when it is present. At some time, everyone feels out of sorts—you may feel like you are suffering from an ailment. Just like when you feel sick, it changes your disposition.

The following coping mechanism is the best I have found, because the negativity is out—and after that, I always feel better. This is an alternative to speaking directly with someone if you feel that your hurt won't be resolved. If you feel that you are unable to create positive change by talking your feelings out directly, then it is best to release them and move yourself away from the negativity. Give the person who has offended you a silent blessing, if you feel you can—but you do not need to expose yourself to negativity of any sort at any time.

Too often someone accepts things not in line with their purpose. You may do this for many reasons, such as giving others the benefit of a doubt due to their circumstances or feeling sorry for another. You will see how others really are when they experience challenging times and handle adversity.

The longer you keep an energy-draining person in your life, the more power you give them over your own happiness. Your happiness is something that you—and only you—should be in charge of.

I have found many of these lessons to be quite difficult—but they aren't meant to be easy. If we are lucky enough, we learn them without causing pain to others. If we do affect others, then it is only right to make amends and atone for our mistakes. The most important thing we need to do is forgive ourselves—otherwise we will enter the endless cycle of feeling unworthy and punishing ourselves for it.

I don't think people really realize the positive or negative effect they have on others. Many people have crossed my path. Some are more memorable than others, but most of them have made an impact. The people I value the most have made the biggest impact.

The most blessed thing to have around you is family and good friends; they keep you grounded and provide a great deal of emotional stability. This can really make a huge difference in your life. It can be the one thing that helps you recognize when change is necessary.

I have found that since I have opened myself completely and allowed more positive input into my mind, there are more positive occurrences. People I hadn't been open to before have become people I now admire—not because something in them changed, but because I changed. It's amazing how something as simple as deciding to present an open attitude to others and perceive from them in a positive way has changed my life. I can't stress this enough.

When I was resistant to certain personalities, my resistance would cause instant friction and dislike, because everyone can sense when others rub them the wrong way. When I decided to change that, it made an instant difference. It was work to create that change, but when I changed, there was a ripple effect; the other person changed as well, and the friction was no longer there. After only a short time, it wasn't work anymore, and surprisingly, I had developed natural camaraderie with the people I originally experienced friction with.

It's amazing how little change is required to completely turn things around and how great the magnitude of the outcome can be. When I look back over times when I have resisted change—and how much more effort I was expending to do that—it seems ridiculous to me now how much time I could have spent enjoying others if I had just practiced a little compassion.

CHAPTER TEN

CONTENTMENT

M y only concern in this life is the quality of it—and I don't mean material things, because I can't take any of that with me when I go. The little moments, when nothing monumental is happening, are the ones that bring me the most happiness within. I want to enjoy being with the people who matter the most to me. That is luxury. That is richness.

Connecting with people on a soul level is inspiring. It's as if someone is touching my heart, even though they aren't physically anywhere near it. Sometimes people don't know it, but the little things they do can take my breath away.

The things you can take with you that have the most impact on you are all your happiest memories and close connections with family and friends

No one thing that someone does touches me deeply, and I wouldn't even be able to tell someone about what triggers those good feelings. Contentment is an emotion that's different for every person. I don't know if I became more emotional after I had my daughter (although it felt like it). I do believe that your heart does expand. But the soul connection I speak of is similar to what is felt during events that make you cry (being proud of someone close, any kind of unexpected achievements, weddings, funerals, etc.). The feeling grasps you, and all of a sudden, you are there, shocked at your own reaction.

Acceptance is something that each of us comes to in our own time. The acceptance I speak of is a form of contentment. When we start to live and view our lives in a more contented state, we are experiencing an acceptance within. It's not acceptance in the sense of "I can't get there from here, so I won't try." Instead, it comes from being satisfied with where you are. I'm not saying you should accept where you are even if you don't like it. Do not ever stop striving for what you want out of life—but do acknowledge where you are now. Look at all of the beautiful things that you have in your life, and be thankful and appreciative of them. Have gratitude for all obstacles you have had the strength to overcome. Obstacles aren't just physical—they are also emotional, and it is just as important to overcome emotional obstacles.

Be proud of all of your accomplishments, big and small—for each of them brings you greater wisdom. If you can appreciate the tiny things in life, then the bigger ones are that much more valuable. My experience so far is that not enough people take the time to be proud of what they've accomplished. They are too focused on what they don't have and what they still want.

Imagine if I made a goal to have something in my life b
way. I finally achieve it, and instead of enjoying my ...
of contentment, I overlook accomplishment and say, "It's not
enough; I want more." I'm not saying you shouldn't want too
much—but take the time to give yourself a pat on the back every
once in a while.

If you rush too quickly through life, you might get to the end and
have regrets for not enjoying certain milestones a little more. You
always hear parents talk about how their kids grew up so fast and
how they missed so many moments and events with them. Take
time to really appreciate moments as they happen—you certainly
won't get them back. It's good to look ahead to the future—but
not to the detriment of missing the present.

It's strange how my own contentment hit me after some quality
time of reflection. It wasn't anything that anyone else could
do. Surprisingly, it was this time of contentment that was very
inspiring and necessary to my own personal growth.

It has taken me a long time to come to this place of contentment.
Instead of responding right away to things that bother me, I now
take the time to think things through fully. If I still feel strongly
about something after my reflection, then I will discuss it—but
most of the time, it's just the effects of others' out-of-balance
behaviors. You can't change others' opinions to suit what you
believe. You must allow others to have their own opinions—just
as you are entitled to yours. It isn't your right to say that you know
all and that your word is the ultimate truth.

There are many things that lead me to believe I have found my
true path which turned out to be writing, not just this book but

to continue writing.—For so long I felt there was something more I should be doing but had no idea what that was until I felt compelled to write. As soon as I started I felt it resonate within my soul and knew I had to continue on this amazing journey. I felt so alive and rejuvenated every time I put a pen in my hand and write and everything flowed so fast. It felt like I hit the path running, and I continue to feel this way more and more each day. All of the signs I've ever had led me to it. I didn't always recognize them, but looking back, now I can see it so clearly. The ups and downs I have experienced had to happen in order for me to reach my true path and potential. This is exactly how others who have found their paths have relayed it as well.

My passion has always been inside me, and when it comes alive, it is completely exhilarating to say the least. I think you know deep down what you passion is—but it seems to be on an unreachable level until you reach the point in your life where you are ready to receive it.

Everyone gets to this point at different times, which is why I say that every person is a unique individual. Each person has their own clock for certain periods of growth in their life; you can't force growth or speed it up. There is no need to worry about what everyone else is doing. Focus on what you are doing and how that relates to your relationships. The outward effect of this will be evident.

Noticing how you feel when you are on your true path is an indication in itself. For me, the feeling of contentment is a surge of energy. It is extremely exhilarating, and it makes me feel so alive. It's how I would imagine I would feel if I had won the lottery—in a way, I have. Not everyone will experien.. ... exact same indicator I do. You have to determine what your indicator is and how to recognize when it's at the beginning stage. If you are unaware, you could easily be diverted and miss the sign altogether, taking you off course for more time than you'd like.

Emotionally, everyone needs a balance. Without balance, your soul can feel undernourished, causing you to take actions that aren't consistent with who you really are. Most of the time, these actions stem from a greater need within—from an area that is depleted. Any emotion can be depleted at any one time. This depletion happens when you have overspent or deprived yourself. Sometimes we don't recognize this until it is too late. Sometimes we don't recognize it at all, and it shows up in how we respond or to others.

Wouldn't it be great if there was some master manual that we could consult—a manual that would give us the prescription for what we need to do when difficult circumstances arise. We do have that manual—it is our own inner wisdom and life experiences. I would have liked it if someone had told me what to do in certain situations—but then the question becomes, *would I have listened?* It's a toss-up on that one—but I'm going to guess not. Every one of us has our own answers within ourselves. It takes a lot of self-reflection to find our answers, but we have the answers already. They call it soul-searching for a reason. But with this fast-paced world of *busy, busy, busy,* we don't often take time for ourselves. That isn't good for us at all. We deserve our own peace and individual time. When you take time for yourself, you will find that you had the answers to your problems all along. It is in those quiet moments that those realizations happen.

When I look back, I can't help but to be thankful for the experiences that created my own transformation.

CHAPTER ELEVEN

INSPIRATION

Inspiration comes in many forms—through people, nature, animals, and other forms.

We will attract what we think about. When I feel like I need inspiration and motivation, I think about how much I would like some of it—and within minutes, I start to feel the emotions I needed and asked for. You have your own guides and helpers. All you need to do is ask, and they will be there, providing you with what you need. In order to receive what you ask for, you need to be open to it. If you are not open to receiving inspiration, there is no way it will get through, and you won't feel any better. It's great to put your faith out there and ask, but if you have a wall up that doesn't allow inspiration in, then you are blocking yourself from all that is available to you.

One of the things I find inspiring is talking with others who also share a positive outlook and a unique perspective. Everyone perceives similar situations and occurrences in a different light. I find it interesting and inspiring to hear other positive perspectives I hadn't considered. Talking with positive people spurs on a snowball effect of inspiration and motivation. The more we talk, the more these positive emotions escalate—almost to the point of overstimulation at times. You can become so motivated about something that if you don't take action within a certain period of time, you lose the momentum you have built within because the inspiring emotions have reached a plateau and you are emotionally worn out. This is similar to the rush and the following crash of an energy drink. If you don't grab the momentum when you have it, you lose it. It is important to continue motivation and inspiration by coupling them with action. This way the cycle will continually build and grow. I've noticed that what might seem insignificant can sometimes be the prelude to inspiration.

The best thing you can do is to get back in touch with nature. This is the root of how everything began. It's so simple; yet sometimes we so easily forget. I am always drawn to water; it seems to be my biggest resource of peace and calm. One of my biggest inspirations to assist my writing is being by the ocean. The sounds are so soothing to my soul; they promote and inspire my creativity.

Sometimes when I have been aware of a mood that's overcome me and I am feeling unsettled from it, I call on the spirits of family members who have passed on. Within minutes, I feel much more at peace. What I feel is love, and it calms and soothes my unsettled emotions. I've also found that inspirational ideas and motivation follow shortly. Notice that the word *spirit* is within the word *inspiration*. To me, this correlation makes sense. The spirit I feel with me the most is that of my maternal grandmother. She was a very strong, wise, and independent-thinking woman. I feel that she is my voice of reason when I feel disconnected. Just thinking about her and remembering how much I loved her inspires me tremendously. If you have someone in your life who you admire in a way that brings inspiration and motivation to you, then try thinking of what their advice might be when you feel unsettled or disconnected. I think it won't be long before you feel better. If you also take action based on what you feel their words of wisdom would be, then all the better.

If nothing else, this change of thoughts distracts your energy; the time it has taken to change the train of thought might have been all the time you needed to alleviate the unsettling emotions that were bothering you. If that doesn't actually change your mindset, then if nothing else it gave your discontent a time-out, which will definitely help you.

Ask yourself what it is that calms and soothes you. You will most likely find that when you are in that state of mind, your creativity and intellect are inspired. Whatever works for you is best. You know inherently what soothes your spirit; yet somehow you deprive yourself of your greatest comfort. I don't think you do this on purpose. I think you do this because you forget, and it seems too simple to acknowledge. In this busy, busy life, you don't take enough opportunity to enjoy the beauty that surrounds you. Do you ever notice how children look at everything so sweetly, with wonderment and awe? It's mostly because they don't have the stresses and responsibilities that adults have, but also because they choose to see things as they really are—in their simplest form. It's so easy for them to appreciate this, but so hard for adults to pay attention; yet this attention to detail is exactly what you need. Why do you always deny yourself? You feel the need to be busy—so busy that you lose your own desires and hamper your own happiness. For some reason, you have this idea that you are supposed to be doing so much. You should watch children and learn more from them. It's strange that the answers are right in front of you—sometimes you just need to look through a child's eyes.

I look at so many things—children and animals, to name a few—and they seem so peaceful and carefree. You may spend a lot of time running around, trying to get everything done so you have the time to sit back and enjoy life's simple pleasures. Why not take the time out now? Life would be so much more enjoyable if you take time out for yourself every once in a while. It's like recharging the batteries that keeps your soul going. Take the time to watch the mild ripple on the water that resonates within your soul, the waves going back and forth on the shore, a butterfly flitting about, the trees blowing in the breeze, the wind on your cheeks, or the sun warming you enough to keep you from feeling cold on a brisk fall day.

Look at all the wonder and beauty that surrounds you, and it will help to quell the inevitable busyness of life. All of these examples follow the basic idea of taking time out to smell the roses. The people who take this time are usually the ones we strive to be like, because they seem the happiest. These people are happy because they know the secret to their souls' peace. Even listening to the rain or watching the snow fall can be peaceful. All these gifts from nature are given to you to rejuvenate your soul. It's not that you don't see or want to enjoy nature's gifts; you are too busy, and you make promises to yourself to enjoy them another day. Sometimes you need to take a particular day and enjoy it. Your body will tell you when you need time for yourself—often you tell it, "Later." This is so crazy! Take time out when your soul really needs it. Listen to your own body; it knows when the time is right. Stop denying yourself life's pleasures for another day—take time to enjoy them now!

I could go on about this, but I think you get the idea. There's enough craziness in this world to distract you, so give yourself a time-out in the present and bask in it. Don't wait for the future. It will happen anyway, and wouldn't you rather get there happy than too worn out—or not make it there at all—because you didn't feed your soul?

I've always found that when I take this much-needed time for myself, I feel the greatest inspiration. It is that time of peace and soul nourishment that I think about all areas of my life—a reflection of sorts. I reflect on where I have come from, where I am going and want to go, what I am going to do now to get me there, and especially on how to enjoy the road on the way. It's like a little catnap to reawaken your soul and provide you with the inspiration and motivation you need to sustain you through your life journey.

Once you become inspired, it is easy to keep the inspiration rolling, because there are no blocks to inhibit you. I'm sure that you have noticed how much progress you can make when you feel inspired and motivated. At times I have been surprised by what I have accomplished.

The same is true for music, art, and anything creative. People are drawn to things that make them happy—something to inspire. Creative outlets can be quite inspiring and can take you to another level—a level you might not have otherwise encountered. When you hear a song on the radio that is upbeat and puts you in a good mood, you feel happy and motivated. Let's say you then let another car in front of you instead of freezing it out, thus starting a chain reaction of good deeds and happy thoughts. What a difference it makes—a small change happens within, and you feel better inside. That's what it is all about.

Most people are looking to be inspired. Why not strive to be one who creates the inspiration you want to evolve? I have noticed that the people who have had the most positive influence on my life are the ones who I respect and admire the most.

When you ask the universe for what you need, it will respond to your request. I've experienced this firsthand, as I have received everything I have ever asked for. The key to all of this is to be specific in what you ask for. Remember to count your blessings along the way. Realize that you should never assume that the universe knows what you're thinking when you ask—like most people, even the universe can't read your mind. If you went to a car lot and you wanted to get a red convertible, would you just assume that the salesperson would know exactly what you wanted if you said you wanted a car? Similarly, the universe needs to know as much as you can give it. I have gotten everything I wanted—but it didn't always come the way I had expected, because sometimes I wasn't specific enough.

For example, if you want to bring people into your life who will be great friends, ask for people to be brought to you who are in alignment with your life's purpose. Always be specific!

CHAPTER TWELVE

INTENTION

Don't ever deny what you want. You can do whatever you want if you put your mind and heart into it. Have you ever noticed how one little event can change your entire direction in life? Why not be the one in charge of changing your direction? Circumstances do that easily enough. Choose to be the one who is in charge of this part of your life. I understand that not all circumstances are within your control—but how you choose to handle them is. I love this phrase: "It's not who you are underneath—it's what you do that defines you." There are so many people in our world who are trying to make a positive difference—and no one is restricted from being one of those people. The only restrictions blocking you are created by you.

It has been my experience that I develop certain reactions to different types of behaviors. In the spirit of practicing what I preach, I had found that it used to take a tremendous amount of control to not react to others' behavior. While it is still difficult not to react at times, I try very hard to be cognizant of my reactions and take an active role in not reacting outwardly, which is the one thing I do have control over. I tend to internalize things until I figure them out. Sometimes it takes longer than I would like, but eventually I work things out. My intention is to learn not to let others affect me in a negative way. Even though this can be hard, I know I can do it.

There are so many opportunities available to you. You just need to choose to see the opportunities and grab hold of them to make changes.

I used to think that I didn't have the resources and was unable to do anything about certain occurrences. Not every positive change has to do with stature, placement, or money. Your contribution to the world could be as simple as being the one person to make someone smile after a month of others overlooking them. Everyone has a contribution they can make—big or small, every contribution matters. There is no world scale out there that will be rating your contributions—your own mind that makes this perception. Every action has a trickle-down effect. You may not see the effect of your actions, but you must believe and have faith that the effects are there.

I have put these restrictions on myself, and it has taken a lot of time for me to realize this. Everyone is here for a reason. Every person makes a contribution. We don't always know or see what our contribution is, but it is there. There are many examples I can give to reinforce this. I will name a few.

If you have someone in your life who you view as being completely intolerable, know that you will develop tolerance. It may not be a huge amount, but it will be the amount you need to navigate your life the way it was intended. I used to have no patience at all. My mother jokes about when I was a child. She still remembers a notebook she got for me. In the corner of each page was a picture of a baby saying, "God grant me patience, but please hurry."

My beautiful daughter was placed in my life to teach me to be patient. I'm sure you're thinking that all children do that. Not everyone learns patience just from having children, but it was exactly the method necessary for me to learn it. Not every person is the same, and we all learn differently. Depending what you're here to learn and evolve from, your lessons will come in the method that will be most effective for you. Learning tolerance and patience was especially essential for me because of the diverse people who were meant to be in my life. The patience I learned from my daughter has taught me how to deal with and appreciate them, as well as learn how to take only the positive aspects of those people.

No well-known person you read about or see on TV knew their path from the beginning. That's the wonderment of life. You could be here to make a change in this world that you could have never predicted. If the lifestyle you currently have doesn't look as pretty as you'd like it to be, you can change that. Life can change drastically in a minute, cascading into a path you never could have imagined. Don't try to steer your ship against the current—instead, try to guide it. The path of least resistance is the path that is easier to travel. Using the analogy of steering a ship, you can't always make a ship go the way you want it to. The saying "you can lead a horse to water, but you can't make it drink" describes the nature of life. Nature is very powerful—much more powerful than we will ever be. If we could control it, then we would have by now. Can we prevent mass disasters of nature? No, we can't. Other changes are just a smaller scale of that same idea. We can only start within and hope that the trickle-down effect takes it from there.

In line with the trickle-down effect, imagine only great things happening in your life. See how this makes you feel inside. When I was writing, I was inspired through solace and peace—and from that peace grew inspiration. The more energy I put into my writing, the happier I became; the happier I became, the better I felt within; and the happier I felt within, the more inspired I felt—this is the trickle-down effect that I created for myself. My trickle-down effect worked for me entirely. I was no longer affected by the negative and only let the positive in, thus creating more and more positive things. Negativity is like darkness; positivity is the light. When there is no room for the negative, it shrinks away, and the positive prevails.

Try to envision good luck and good things happening. No dream is too big to accomplish. Every material object in this world started as a thought—an idea that grew into being before you. Imagine this for a moment—the person who created shelter started out with an idea. Could they make it happen? If you can think it, you can create it! In a quick version of this, the beginnings of a crude shelter grew to be a house, and then houses escalated into buildings. Now imagine if the one person who had the thought to create shelter could see what it has escalated to today. Never put a ceiling on yourself, or you will surely seal your fate and keep yourself stuck a perpetual cycle of inhibited growth.

Live each day as it happens. Live in the present. This is a task I myself have struggled with at times.

It's hard not to think about or be concerned with your future. The more time you put into thinking about the future, the less time you are left with in the present. Let's say you spend twenty-five percent of your time thinking or worrying about the future—that means only seventy-five percent of your mind is available for the present.

What if an opportunity comes along that is perfect for you but you miss it because you were distracted by thoughts about the future? We're trained to think about the future from the time we are children. Questions are always asked of us like, "What do you want to be when you grow up?" This teaches us that we need to be thinking about the future. But thoughts of the future don't need to consume us. Luckily, children don't concentrate much of their time on this, because children live in the present. A child's daily questions have to do with what house everyone will play at, where the sleepover is, what's for lunch, etc.

As we get older, we start to plan what we want to do and at what age we expect to accomplish something. Then as time goes by, we start to stress about how much time we have left based on time constraints we made as a teenager. How reliable were we as teenagers with regard to our future and making plans? I know I wasn't very likely to have made good choices back then. Yes, there were students I went to school with who had real goals and worked hard to make them happen. I now consider them to be the elite ones, because they knew what they wanted. But most teenagers are struggling to find their place in this world. I was one of the ones who didn't have a clue where to look.

As time passes, if you have passed an age-related goal you have set for yourself, then this can lead to panic, more time spent thinking about the goal, and pressuring yourself about the future. When you do this, the present suffers—and so do you. You can't imagine how much more I started to enjoy each day as it came when I was no longer worrying and pressuring myself about the future.

The future is inevitable; it will happen no matter what. It's okay to have plans for the future. But the only way to have a future is to live in the present and take the steps needed to have that future. Be fully present in your own life, always pay attention to the greater purpose, and never deny yourself what you know you can achieve.

How can you see what's going on around you when you can't even look up to notice your life as it unfolds in front of your own eyes? You may say, "Everything is too busy, and I will enjoy life next week or next month." What happens when next week or next month doesn't come—or three months have gone by already? You have to enjoy the little moments, not save them for later. Every once in a while, you need to take pause, pay attention, and appreciate the moment.

Whatever you need to do to soothe your soul is what you should do now. Don't wait! Start living your life with purpose, with the intent of making life around you glorious in all aspects. You will see that when you change, others will change around you. You will find that life will be more enjoyable. Your life will not be the crazy daily grind that it is now; it will ultimately be happier.

When you are happy, others will be affected by your mood in a positive way. I would much rather live happily and be less burned out then be weighed down by negativity and discord.

There is so much in this life that is sad and depressing. I don't want to have any negativity in my life at all. If I focus on the negative, it will continue to grow. Do you ever notice that when you are in a great mood, great things keep happening? That's why you hear people say things like, "This day just keep getting better." That is because they are happy, focused, and open to positive occurrences. That focus grows, creating more and more happiness. Then there's the opposite—one bad thing happens in a day, and bad things just snowball from there. If you don't let go of the first bad thing, the trickle-down effect continues.

Make a decision to not allow negativity in. Change the atmosphere around yourself. It's your decision whether to let negativity affect you. Only *you* are responsible for your own happiness. Life is what *you* make it. If you want a certain job, go out and get it. If you want food or clothes, go out and get them. If you want love, you are open to receive it. Without your initiative, good things won't happen. Why would you expect someone else to create your happiness? *You* are the one who knows what truly makes you happy, so you need to be the one to create your happiness. Everything worth having is worth working for, and when you work hard to create something, you can appreciate it that much more. If everything was just handed to you, you wouldn't value things as deeply. I have been very blessed in my life, and the things I appreciate the most are the ones I could never buy. The most beautiful things in life are immaterial—and yet some people define themselves by what they have. You can't take anything with you when you are gone. If a person has achieved great wealth but is mean-spirited, how likely are you to be friends with them? How much happiness can a person buy if they have no one to share their happiness with? When you are happy or sad, you feel it in your heart; no amount of money can change that.

Emotional attachments are what a person seeks in life. You need someone to connect with, fulfill you, and warm your heart—whether through friendship or passionate love. It is that love that sustains you through difficult times. Create love, have faith, and believe in that magic—I do. I can't always see or feel love, but I experience happiness from that faith alone. Believe in good luck, and that belief will grow. If you believe you are lucky, you will be lucky; if you believe you are unlucky, you will be successful in that belief as well.

Treat others as you would like to be treated; don't ever compromise that. If you treat others badly, you are committing treason against your heart and soul which will cause you more pain than you can ever inflict on others. You will find that the happier you are, the happier you will become. Not everyone wants to feel happiness. Some people say they want to be happy, but if they do nothing to attain it or keep their happiness, then they still have their own inner issues to work on.

Others will either be drawn to you or move away from you. Negativity cannot survive in a positive environment. If others don't want to or can't let go of negativity, they are more likely to move away from you, which is good. Some people choose to embrace negativity—not necessarily because they want to, but because it is a familiar shield to hide behind. This is a sad reality, but if you find you are doing this, then it is necessary for your own happiness to find a way to let go of this soul-damaging emotion.

New, positive experiences will fill the void of negativity, and you will feel much more alive. With each day that passes, positive feelings will grow. Yes, there will be days when you will digress; everyone has those blue days. The trick is to recognize when it happens and figure out what triggered the negativity. The best way I have found to counteract this is to remind myself of all the beautiful things I have to be thankful for. Sometimes it can be hard to pull yourself out of this, but hopefully you have people in your life who can help carry you through when times feel rough. Try not to give in to the process of negative thinking. You don't need or deserve negativity in your life. You deserve to be happy!

I will tell you this as many times as I need to, because I want you to really and truly believe it. You are an important part of this universe. Everyone comes here with a gift. Whether your gift is big or small, it's still a gift. If you don't already know with your gift is, try to discover what it. Discovering your gift is important.

Never let anyone tell you that you don't matter or that what you think doesn't matter. If something matters to you, it matters! There are some truly phenomenal human beings out there. Some people have discovered what their gifts are, and some haven't. Don't you want to be one of the people who know their gifts?

In the end, you are the true judge of yourself. You are the only one who has the power to change who you are if you don't like yourself. Many of the people I encounter are looking for some form of personal growth, and I think that is why we are always striving to reach a higher form of living.

We can't give someone enough opportunity to help them create change. A person has to want change for themselves. I have found that the best thing to do for someone else is pray for help—that they will be the person they are meant to be. The universe will give them the opportunity, and it's up to them if they take it.

At the end of this, I only have one question that I would really like for you to contemplate:

What do *you* really want from this life? What do *you* want to do? When you dig deep to find these answers, it can be very liberating and rewarding. Don't use any excuse to prevent yourself from achieving what you want. The only thing that prevents you from achieving what you want is yourself.

This is why you always hear others say, "If anyone had told me two (or three, or five) years ago that this is where I would be, I never would have believed them."

This is a great example of how things can change. Sometimes things change quickly, and sometimes not as quickly. But if your life changed drastically over the course of two to five years, wouldn't that seem quick when you looked back?

Imagine how those changes—the ones you absolutely wanted—happening, how happy you would be, and how great you would feel.

Anything can be changed around to what you want. The key is to know what you really want deep down and go after it. If you put your mind to it, you can accomplish anything you want.

We are all unique and have all developed to be who we are due to our environments and the events in our lives. The challenge of life is to learn and grow from each of these.

The fact that you have chosen to read this book and others like mine is a positive step in the direction of your own soul-searching. When you actively seek out the tools needed to elevate yourself, you will be closer to your true self—and that will create a lot of happiness within.

You alone will lead the way to your true path and desires. You will discover a life with greater meaning, contentment, and purpose. This exact search brought me to my true path and desires I didn't realize were there.

It was surprising to me how long it took for me to search for what my purpose was and what made me truly happy. I had spent so much time ensuring that others around me were taken care of and happy that I had neglected myself severely. Even more surprising was that the people I had chosen to take care of were nowhere around to return the TLC.

This led me on a whole other search for true meaning, finding my own abilities, trusting myself, and trusting the people I had put my faith in. My search challenged all the standards I had set for myself and others. I realized how much of myself I had sacrificed to make others happy. This may sound like a rant or like I feel sorry for myself—but it turned out to be the opposite. Once I came to this level in my life, I realized that the true cause for not knowing what I wanted and needed was my own self-neglect.

I wasn't taking true care of myself. I hadn't set high enough limits on how others should treat me. I hadn't taken time to ask myself what I really wanted—time I had given others. The person I most needed to take care of was myself. I had been avoiding and neglecting myself for too long. When I finally realized that, I started to change. I found that I was happier, and others around me began to see and experience that happiness. In taking care of myself, I was also taking better care of others because of what I was reflecting outwards. When you start to take care of yourself, you reflect inner happiness. That inner happiness will attract people to you who will be more reflective of your true soul. In a sense, it is like taking off the rose-colored glasses and seeing others for who they truly are, what they really want, and what they have to offer you. I found that I surrounded myself with the people who were not in alignment with who I was and wanted to become. These people were taking much-needed happiness from my life.

I discovered that I was a fix-it type of person. I was eternally drawn to emotionally challenged and broken people who I could help—and some of these people were savvy enough to realize that they could take advantage of that.

What determines who you will become is the environment in which you were raised and now live in. To determine this, you need to take a good look at what has molded you to be who you are today. What are the unique circumstances that created the person you are now? What people have been in your life, what people are still in your life, and how has each person played a unique role in your personal development?

Your true path is something that your soul knows instinctively, but that you as a human with an overactive ego don't always know. Picture your path as being a straight or winding road. It doesn't matter which road you choose, and every time you are deterred or stray from the path, the people you meet and events that occur are the markers that will serve as reminders. Whether you make mistakes or experience personal triumph, these markers remind you of what you have come through and learned.

At times, you will come back across the markers that were difficult. Those markers will remind you that you are in danger of straying from your true path again, or possibly that you are heading to a place of guilt, shame, or dismay. Either way, when you encounter memories, you may find that they inspire hope and faith and encourage you to remember that if nothing else, you have learned and grown. Even though some are disappointing and difficult, they are significant and necessary.

Everyone is unique, and everyone's soul's desire is unique. I am surprised by the number of people who believe there is one route in life and that if everyone isn't on that route, then there is something wrong with them. A good example of this is our own programming from childhood.

Most of us are raised with the idea that we are to grow up, get a good job, get married, have kids, etc. Now why should that apply to everyone? If we are unique individuals, then our lives should be unique as well. No two lives are alike; therefore, the "one route" that most abide by doesn't apply.

Your soul will be content with what matches your soul's desire. Not everyone's soul desires are the same, but if any one person isn't striving for just their desires in that order, then others think that something must have happened along the way and that they are off their path.

CHAPTER THIRTEEN

DETERMINING YOUR WEAKNESSES

I have found that when I am bothered by change or the way that someone has responded to me, it causes me to invite negativity into my life, whether through my thoughts or actions. Everything has a trickle-down effect. It is just defined by the root that trickle-down effect , whether positive or negative. If I choose to acknowledge the negative, then my behavior changes in a negative way, which doesn't really do any good for me or those around me. I realize that it can be extremely difficult to shrug this off sometimes, especially when others are behaving negatively toward you. However, others' actions could also be caused by the trickle-down effect of the person who infected them. If my reaction to a negative person is also negative, I am likely to behave as they have. The negative person is already feeling awful, which is why they are acting outwardly. It doesn't make me feel any better to also act out.

I can create a positive change if I respond positively. People are more likely to step back and reevaluate their own behavior if I don't come back to them with the same negative attitude that they are dishing out.

The people who have made the biggest difference in my life are the ones who have promoted positive change. I have never been drawn to negativity; most people aren't. Those who have experienced great hurt and disappointment are most likely emanating negativity—not through any fault of their own except that they have been hurt and have not had enough positive reinforcement around them or enough self-confidence to counteract the negativity or help them deal with it in a positive way. I'm not saying that negativity is something we have to tolerate, but we can at least be aware of it and have the wisdom to realize that everyone has their own issues to deal with and learn from. A negative person just hasn't come to a place of contentment, and responding negatively doesn't do anything for anyone.

My tendency has always been to take things much too personally and react in a very oversensitive way.

Suppose I have an interaction with someone that disappoints or a person is disrespectful to me. I then form an opinion about that person based on their behavior. Someone else comes along who behaves even worse, and this helps to diminish my previously formed opinion of the other person so that it is at the level it should have originally been.

What I mean by this is that sometimes people overreact. In moments of hurt and disappointment, they overestimate the impact of others. This isn't a good thing to do, but I think many people have been guilty of this at one time or another. Your ego is in a constant fight with your soul.

Everything happens for a reason. Sometimes you learn a lesson when you make unnecessary and unfair judgments. What ends up happening is that you draw more of unnecessary and unfair judgments from others into your life to teach you lessons.

I didn't always resist all my personal growth lessons, but I did resist some in the past. Since experiencing and accepting that changes inevitably happen, I find that I live a much more contented life. I still have moments when I might react or resist to negative actions, but I've found that these times are becoming less frequent.

Awareness is power! As I learn to recognize the signals in my body and spirit, I learn to counteract and deflect them. I am much more comfortable with contented behavior. I don't have any desire for negativity; I'm sure most people don't. However, it's surprising how many people welcome negativity and resist the natural flow of their own soul's evolution.

The key to deflecting negativity is learning to recognize your own triggers within your self. No two people are the same, which is why no problem has just one solution. In the world of spirit, there is no "one size fits all."

This is all part of the karmic debt we have created through each life lived. Karma is not something you create for yourself with expectations of good or bad karma. Every action has a trickle-down effect into your own personal karma. The lessons we are here to learn so that we may experience personal growth are all part of the karma that has been created through our past lives.

Whether the karma is good or bad will be evident to us. For example, your tough current life could be the result of karmic debt from the past, as well as the lessons you have chosen to learn for your own soul progression. The karmic debt may also have been paid up, and you may be able to finally relax in the tranquility of peace in your later years.

Some people repeat the same mistakes—and this is only because these people resist the lessons they should learn. Their resistance usually results in more bad choices, and these bad choices may build their karmic debt bank even more.

My example of this is my own, which I find to be liberating I spent the majority of my life trying to make everyone else's life easier, but their lives did not become easier and therefore my effort was not reciprocated. However, when I finally started to pay more attention to my needs, take a stand, and take care of myself first, needy people weren't in my life as often. Some people are givers, and some are takers. When there is not an even balance of give and take, the people who ask only "What can you do for me?" will move elsewhere.

I was stunned by how many people I knew turned out to be concerned only with what I could give them. These people were meant to be in my life until I learned the very lessons necessary that took me where I was meant to be as an individual. The surprising thing was that I had become more aware of my needs on a soul level. My awareness enabled me to grow as I needed. My awareness allowed me to open and take notice of selfish people before I allowed them to enter my life.

Upon learning that lesson, I developed boundaries that I should have had in place long before. I found that others had become accustomed to being able to control how I reacted and behaved. Those who had controlled me were stumped; they seemed to feel bewildered because they were no longer able to control me.

I became stronger in my mind and my will. This strength was a huge benefit and a trait I required to go forth into the future that was meant for me. If I was too easily swayed, as before, then I would never succeed in what was meant to be. Everything happens for a reason. Even when I am in the darkness of a lesson and think there is no benefit to whatever heartache I am going through, I need to remember my strength, trust, and have faith that I need the lesson and that the reason for it will eventually become evident.

When I am experiencing especially tough lessons, I realize that my future is of great importance and responsibility for me. I can say without a doubt that I have experienced unique and challenging lessons—but the rewards have far outweighed the heartache that at times accompanied the lessons .

CHAPTER FOURTEEN

RECOGNIZING YOUR TRIGGERS

Everyone is unique, and everyone has their own triggers. It is up to you to assess your lessons, learn from them, and experience personal growth. Without the growth, you don't evolve and become the person we are meant to be. You may not know what you are meant to do in this life, but all the events in your life prepare you for and lead you to your purpose. If you do not learn and progress through the challenges in front of you, then you may not reach your full potential. The result will be that you are thwarting your own progression, happiness, and success.

I know that I am sensitive and easily affected by others' words and actions. This is the reason all my lessons were difficult—but they were necessary, as I am sensitive by nature.

It's interesting to watch groups of people to see how they interact with one another. If you pay close attention, you can identify which role each person in the group plays. There may be an instigator—one who gets others revved up just for the fun of it. There may be a person who is aggressive and responds to the instigator. Others may be passive and just watch; there might also be a mediator. Which type of person are you?

My view of these four types of people used to be quite limited, but experience has taught me to see everything in the bigger picture. Even though some people may seem insignificant to you, they do have a greater purpose, and each of them can play a significant role in your life.

For example, an instigator can teach you tolerance; an agitator can teach you patience. If you are trying to be the mediator too often, then maybe the instigator and agitator are in your life to teach you that not every battle is yours; therefore, the lesson is one of moderation. As for the passive crowd, it's possible that the lesson is to become stronger in their standards. I'm not saying that these are the exact lessons before you. You know where your weaknesses in your relations with others, and with some deep soul-searching, you can usually figure out what role you are playing and learn from it. Each person is totally different. However, people are all alike in that we are all here to experience, learn, and grow. Recognizing what triggers certain reactions within you is the key to having a healthier existence.

I try to be passive most of the time. It doesn't do me any good to get worked up over topics that aren't as important to me as others. If I feel strongly about an important subject, then I will stand up for it. I pick my battles. You will find your own balance—a comfort level to work with.

It has taken me a long time to recognize when I am stepping onto the wrong path emotionally, and equally as long to learn how to divert from that path. Luckily I have been blessed with a great family and friends who have always offered me strong support. Their support has made my road much more tolerable. Without these people in my life, I would have still ended up with the same mindset and outlook on life—but I know that with these special people in my life, my journey has been faster and I have felt less alone.

Ultimately, this learning is something that needs to be accomplished by you. This is why you sometimes feel alone. However, the placement of great support in your life helps make it bearable and gives you the strength to go through it. That's why it's so important to make sure you acknowledge all contributions by others. Other people are in your life for a reason. It's not totally necessary to know the reason someone is in your life, but it is necessary to acknowledge them. Without the people in your life, you may not have learned a very important lesson.

One of my biggest personal obstacles is patience. I have developed the ability to have patience for other people. My challenge comes in the form of the value of my own personal time. I have always been a very busy person. I am busy in my life and in my mind; therefore, impatience rears its ugly head when the time I have allotted for every occurrence in my life is infringed upon. The best solution for me is to not commit to having too much on my plate—which brings me to one of my other struggles, which is trying to meet everyone else's needs to the detriment of my own sanity. While it is honorable to be considerate of others and their needs, it should never sacrifice your own needs. When you deprive your own soul of its inner desires and needs, it will affect you (and the people around you) negatively.

We often rush so quickly through our lives that we don't take the time to pay attention to what others are saying. Everyone out there is just looking to make soul connections with others. Those connections help to fulfill you in even the most trivial ways. Don't discount someone because you think they don't have anything important to say. Instead, listen, pay attention, and treat that person the way you would like to be treated. It's not for you to decide what should be important to others or what they should talk about. If someone feels something is important enough to talk about, then you can be polite and give them the respect and attention they deserve—no matter what your opinion is. This is basic respect for others, and it is something that our society needs to revisit. This busy, busy world is diminishing a lot of our basic values.

I learn something from everyone I encounter. I don't always learn information that is crucial to my evolution, but I can learn something from everyone I meet.

The placement of everyone in your life plays an important role. The events of your life sometimes lead you off your path—and then lead you back on it again. There are no coincidences; even small things are significant.

You will notice that when you are not in alignment, you experience varying degrees of negativity; you may also experience roadblocks. Pay attention to the signals your body gives you to let you know when you are off your path. An example of a signal is anger at things that wouldn't normally bother you.

My path has been long and arduous, and I have had many hard lessons to learn.

Emotionally hitting rock bottom is the equivalent of a dark night of the soul. If you have difficulty with certain attributes you possess, then this dark night can be the necessary turning point you might need. When you hit rock bottom, you reevaluate everything. If you reach rock bottom, then obviously the reevaluation was necessary.

If you are not learning the lessons in life that you set out to learn, then drastic times call for drastic measures. The universe will create something drastic to get your attention. It is at this point that you finally connect to your innermost desires and steer yourself back on the path to your true self. It is at this point that you need to thank the universe for all it has brought you.

Think back in your life and see if you can pick out events that you thought were insignificant at the time, but that ultimately had a place in bringing you to where you are today. It's an interesting and insightful exercise, and you will find a few occurrences that led you to where you are today. You will be amazed at what you had deemed insignificant; I know I was.

I was extremely hard on myself for not realizing the significance of many things at the time. I tend to set the standards for myself too high at times. I had high expectations for myself and did not have high expectations for others. This has been a constant struggle for me to overcome.

Anyone who can figure out the ultimate reason for events that happen—especially sad ones—is lucky. There are not many people who can do this. When people go through difficult times, it is very beneficial to talk things through with others who can offer an objective opinion. That is what helps keep us grounded and sane.

We are a community of people who have a common purpose. We are all here to learn lessons. We also serve as the catalyst for others' lessons.

Your life is similar to a road map. You encounter mileposts—people or occurrences that either temporarily deter you off your path or reinforce your sense of direction. You don't actually get to see the map, so you don't really know where you're going.

I think everyone has down times—times when a person's body tells them it's time to rest and recharge. You may wonder, *what's wrong with me?* But after a day or two, you snap out of it. The placement of the planets plays a role as well. Do you ever notice how odd people are when there is a full moon? Your mood is also guided by planetary movement and placement.

During down times, your soul is regenerating itself—preparing for some change, big or small. When I have experienced these periods of regeneration, they have been the prelude to some enlightening, significant, and welcome change.

People are becoming more conscious of their ability to regenerate and are making great efforts to create positive change. It is very inspiring to see this, because it brings hope and restores faith. All is not lost. We are regaining our basic values. Not everyone has lost their basic values; however, some people have fallen by the wayside.

Another positive effect of these changes is the number of positive events that are occurring. When the people of the world work together, positive things happen, like cures, advancements, community, etc. These things happen as a direct result of world learning. More and more people want to experience and create positive change. This is very noticeable. There has been an increase of the promotion of this kind of lifestyle.

People are becoming more open to positive change, and that creates the opening for more and more change to evolve. The fact that more people are talking and writing about positive change is a direct sign that people are opening themselves up to it. The more people open up and welcome positive change into their lives, the more the positive change will flow.

Like attracts like. You can create whatever you want in your life. You can attract whatever you want through your thoughts. All you need to do is look back on your own life. Remember what you were thinking at certain times and how those thoughts created the outcomes.

Think back, and you will see that things have gone exactly as you have thought (you have created the outcome). When I first looked back on my life, I thought that things turned out differently from the actual outcome. After taking a more in-depth look back, I realized that even though I wanted things to go a certain way, my thoughts guided the way they actually went.

You may be able to fool your conscious mind, but you can't fool your subconscious thoughts. Not everything goes the way you want, your thoughts don't always change that, you have to believe it subconsciously and in your soul. Everything happens for a reason. You might not know the reason at the time, but it usually becomes clear to you later when we have an *aha* moment and realize that even though an occurrence didn't make you happy at the time, it had an underlying reason and lesson.

There are many events I can look back on and think, *that's not what I wanted to happen.* However, I looked back again and realized the greater purpose of the events in my life. You can't always see the lessons and growth in your life right away. Sometimes it takes time to see the greater purpose. But eventually, at the right time, you will figure out the greater meaning of your life. That is the *aha* moment. I love those moments, because they bring me peace, understanding, and a new sense of direction.

It's amazing how much you can learn from children. Children don't yet have adult responsibilities, stress, or a jaded outlook on life. A child's view is still fresh and new. You could benefit from this fresh perspective. You may not realize that even the presence of a child in your life and the challenges or struggles of that child may ultimately teach you as well. A child may teach you something you might not have learned otherwise. These teachings are signs and gifts to become aware of. You should also look to your parents, siblings, friends, etc. for opportunities for growth that can become your lessons, too.

If you are arrogant enough to think that your opinion of someone else means you are right and can't learn anything from that person, then you are cutting yourself off from a perspective on life that you would most likely benefit from.

This book is about finding your own balance and what works best for you. Your path will be different from everyone else's, because no two people are alike. That is what makes us all so unique. It is this blend that makes up our diverse society. Of course, there will be difficulty within this blend. If life had no difficulty, it would be very predictable. Even though some people fear change, predictability can be confining and mundane.

Please take all that resonates within you from this book—whatever works for your own happiness.

God bless.